MINECRAFT™

MOJANG

ONLINE SAFETY FOR YOUNGER FANS
Spending time online is great fun! Here are a few simple rules to help younger fans stay safe and keep the internet a great place to spend time:
- Never give out your real name – don't use it as your username.
- Never give out any of your personal details.
- Never tell anybody which school you go to or how old you are.
- Never tell anybody your password except a parent or a guardian.
- Be aware that you must be 13 or over to create an account on many sites. Always check the site policy and ask a parent or guardian for permission before registering.
- Always tell a parent or guardian if something is worrying you.

Copyright © 2016 by Mojang AB and Mojang Synergies AB. MINECRAFT is a trademark or registered trademark of Mojang Synergies AB.

All rights reserved.

☒MOJANG

Written by Stephanie Milton.
Illustrations by Joe McLaren.

Published in the United States by Del Rey, an imprint of Random House, a division of Penguin Random House LLC, New York.

DEL REY and the HOUSE colophon are registered trademarks of Penguin Random House LLC.

Originally published in hardcover in the United Kingdom by Egmont UK Limited.

ISBN 978-0-399-59320-8

Printed in China on acid-free paper by RR Donnelley Asia Printing Solutions.

randomhousebooks.com

9 8 7 6 5 4 3 2 1

First U. S. Edition

MINECRAFT

MOJANG

NE RECTE

DEORSUM

SUFFODITO

THE SURVIVORS' BOOK OF SECRETS

DEL REY · NEW YORK

CONTENTS

BRIEFING

SEMPER PARATUS

ALWAYS PREPARED

DIRECTIVE

This book contains the collective knowledge of the Survivors.

Who are the Survivors? We're an underground group of survival experts who have been around since the early days of Alpha. Our objectives? To find cunning new ways to deal with hostile mobs and enemy players. To survive longer than anyone else. To be the best.

You're probably wondering why you've never heard of us. It's because we're THAT good. We're experts at covert ops. Misdirection is our middle name. We're invisible right up until the moment we want you to see us.

Our activities are numerous: ops to eliminate growing threats, surveillance missions to assess potential new settlement locations, base development, large-scale weapons production, practical munitions training, hand-to-hand combat and group raids. And that's just our mornings.

Our successes are undeniably impressive: we've battled the Overworld mobs, dealt with enemy factions, set up bases in the Nether and defeated the ender dragon multiple times.

Around here I'm known as The Chief—leader and founding member of the Survivors. I've documented our experiences so we can pass our knowledge on to the next generation. The following pages contain our most cunning plans and our most ingenious inventions. We may be young, but don't let our age mislead you; we've been stuck between a block and a hard place more times than we can count, and always manage to dig ourselves out.

The fact that you even discovered this book tells us that you have the potential to make it—we hid it well to be sure that only the most deserving would find it. Congratulations—you are now the proud owner of the definitive guide to survival. Study it carefully, let it inspire you and you might just stay alive as long as we have.

The Chief

THE CHIEF

CONVENTIONAL WEAPONS AND ARMOUR
A SURVIVAL EXPERT'S ESSENTIALS

Survival rule number one: make lots of weapons. Swords, bows and arrows are a survival expert's essentials, and enchanting them will make them stronger.

ENCHANTMENTS
Unbreaking will increase the lifespan of bows and swords, saving you time and resources. We also recommend fire aspect for swords, to set your enemy on fire, and punch for your bows, to increase the knockback.

ARROWS
A lot of people don't know this, but the spectral arrow is life-changing. Shoot it at your enemy and they'll be outlined in an eerie, glowing light, allowing you to track their movements with ease. They're crafted from a regular arrow and glowstone dust, which means a trip to the Nether, but it'll be worth it when you meet a creeper in a dark cave or on a midnight emergency resource run.

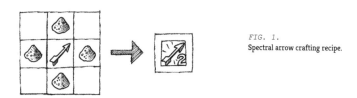

FIG. 1.
Spectral arrow crafting recipe.

Give your arrows a deadly upgrade—tip them with harmful potions to deal even more damage. You can choose from poison, weakness, harming and slowness. Just combine eight arrows and the lingering potion in your crafting grid. These effects can last for up to three minutes—more than long enough to do some damage.

ARMOUR

First impressions are critical; show your enemy who they're dealing with by kitting yourself out in a full set of enchanted diamond armour. This doesn't just give you maximum protection, it sends a message that you're both knowledgeable and in possession of the best materials.

Use your shield to make a personal statement—combine it with your favorite banner and it'll help you cultivate an overall air of impressiveness.

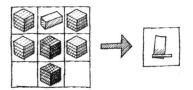

FIG. 2.
Shield recipe. All you need is an iron ingot and wood planks.

You'll slow to sneaking pace when using a shield, but we've found that it reduces melee attacks to 33% and projectiles do no damage at all, so it's a small price to pay.

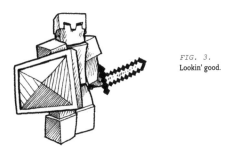

FIG. 3.
Lookin' good.

PRACTICAL MUNITIONS
WHAT TO DO WHEN YOU HAVE NO ACTUAL WEAPONS

Things don't always go to plan, and sometimes you'll be unable to craft a new sword or replenish your stock of arrows when you need to. At moments like these, the art of practical munitions can save your life. This involves some initiative on your part—you'll need to take non-combat materials from your immediate environment and turn them into deadly weapons.

WATER BUCKET
A simple water bucket can knock your opponents backwards, buying you valuable time to make a run for it.

FISHING ROD
Caught off guard on a fishing expedition? Use your rod to knock your attacker backwards, then hook them like a fish and drop them over a cliff or into lava to get rid of them.

FIG. 4.
Successful employment of fishing rod to deal with zombie.

CHICKEN EGGS
Light on weapons and in possession of too many baking ingredients? Use your chicken eggs to knock attackers backwards. Keep a slot free in your inventory so you can collect the eggs you find on your travels—they turn up in the unlikeliest of places.

SNOWBALLS

In snowy areas you can craft snowballs and use them to knock attackers backwards. If you don't live in a snowy biome, invest in a snow golem to ensure you have a constant supply of snow. Craft it from two blocks of snow and a pumpkin head, shut it in a room in your base and pick up the trail of snow it leaves as it shuffles around.

FIG. 5.
Snow golem in residence at the
Survivors' Secret Base.

SAND AND GRAVEL

Stuck in a desert with no wood to craft new weapons? Catch your enemy off-guard with a falling sand trap. You'll need to lure them to your chosen spot, remove any supporting blocks (torches work well for this) and let your sand fall. This trick also works with gravel.

FIG. 6.i
Enemy in position underneath
large quantity of sand supported
by torches.

FIG. 6.ii
Torches removed, enemy buried
in sand.

If you ever find yourself on the receiving end of an ambush like this one, place a torch or button on the block to the side of your head to break the falling sand and give you space to breathe.

WEAPONS ACCESS AND STORAGE

Scrabbling around in your inventory, desperately searching for the right potion mid-battle, isn't going to impress anybody. You must be agile and responsive at all times.

INVENTORY LAYOUT
This inventory layout is used by all of the Survivors—it's proved practical and easy to navigate. Items are grouped together logically and always stored in the same area of the inventory. The most important items are given priority and sit in allocated hotkey slots. Memorize the layout so you'll be able to select what you need as quickly as possible.

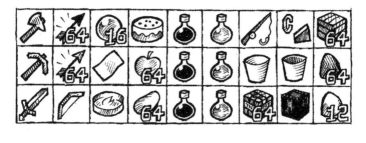

FIG. 7.
Optimum inventory layout as endorsed by the Survivors.

ENDER CHESTS

And now for one of our personal favorite storage solutions—ender chests. They're a great way to keep yourself equipped when you're far away from your base—open one up in the field and you'll have access to the items stored in another ender chest back at your base. They also have a high blast resistance so explosions won't damage them. They're painfully expensive to make, requiring an eye of ender and obsidian, but are worth the investment as they effectively double the size of your inventory. Place ender chests in strategic locations away from your base, or just carry one with you so you can access it wherever you are. And don't worry, even if someone finds your chest, nobody but you will be able to access your items.

Remember, when mining an ender chest, make sure your pickaxe is enchanted with silk touch or you'll lose the eye of ender and only get the obsidian back.

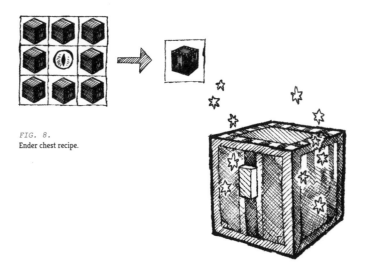

FIG. 8.
Ender chest recipe.

COMBAT ON THE
HOME FRONT

SI VIS
PACEM
PARA BELLUM

IF YOU WANT PEACE, PREPARE FOR WAR

If you're going to survive long-term you'll need a safe place from which to run your operations. But what kind of base is best? It depends on your location and objectives. You'll need to work with the environment you find yourself in. You'll need more space if you're part of a team, but bigger isn't always better if you want to keep off the radar.

There's a lot to think about, so don't rush your decision. The following plans will help you weigh up the pros and cons of six basic base types.

1. GROUND-LEVEL BASE

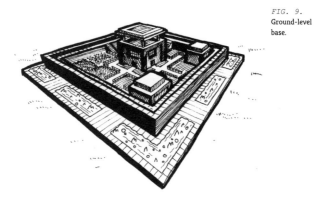

FIG. 9.
Ground-level
base.

PROS:
- Ground level is the most convenient place to build a base.
- You can easily gather resources from the surrounding landscape and see your enemies approaching.

CONS:
- They are impossible for your enemies to miss.

- Unless properly defended, they don't present much of an access challenge for unwelcome visitors.

If you choose a ground-level base, the best location is on a small island, surrounded by water but close to the mainland so you can still access resources.

2. TREEHOUSE BASE

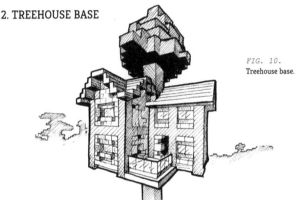

FIG. 10.
Treehouse base.

PROS:
- You'll have the higher ground and a bird's-eye view of the area so it'll be easier to spot approaching enemies.
- They're more difficult to raid than ground-level bases.

CONS:
- They're fairly easy for your enemies to spot.
- They're more difficult for you to access.
- If a hostile mob manages to get up there you may find yourself cornered, and enemy players may use fire to smoke you out.

If you choose a treehouse base, find the largest, tallest tree you can—preferably a jungle tree—as mobs are less likely to spot you. Make sure you have an exit strategy for emergencies.

13

3. SKY BASE

FIG. 11.
Sky base.

PROS:
- You have the high ground and are almost untouchable, as long as your access points are controlled.
- They're ideal if you're likely to suffer frequent attacks as they'll slow your enemies down or put them off completely.

CONS:
- They can be difficult and time-consuming to build as you'll need to tower your way up and down.
- They're removed from useful resources.

If you choose a sky base, make sure it's positioned away from tall trees, mountains or other high ground. Your enemies may take advantage of this and find a way to access your base.

4. UNDERGROUND BASE

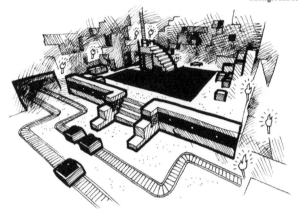

FIG. 12.
Underground base.

PROS:
- They're covert and difficult for enemies to find, unless they know where to look.
- You automatically collect resources as you create an underground base (e.g. valuable ores found exclusively at the bottom of the world), since you'll be undertaking a fair bit of mining.
- If you build your base right at the bottom of the world you can use the bedrock layer for the floor. This ensures nobody can tunnel in underneath you.

CONS:
- It's difficult to keep an eye on what's going on above ground so you may not see your enemies coming.
- They require a lot of mining to construct.
- It's difficult to quickly return to the surface.

If you choose an underground base, experiment with pistons to make an elevator which will carry you up to the surface. Create a hidden point of entry for your elevator at ground level.

5. OCEAN BASE

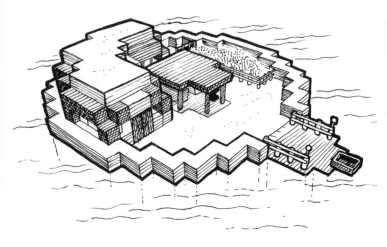

FIG. 13.
Ocean base.

PROS:
- They're difficult to get to unless you have a boat and know what you're looking for.
- You'll be much safer from most hostile mobs in an ocean environment.

CONS:
- They're removed from resources so you'll be making lots of trips back to the mainland.
- They're difficult to access.

If you choose an ocean base, invest in some boats. They'll get you to land more quickly than swimming and are cheap and simple to craft—you just need wood planks.

6. UNDERWATER BASE

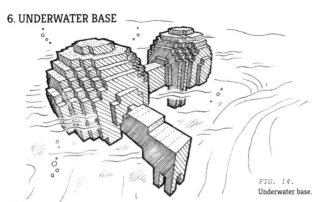

FIG. 14.
Underwater base.

PROS:
- Unless you're followed, your enemy is highly unlikely to locate an underwater base.
- Land-dwelling hostile mobs won't be able to get at you.
- They're impervious to TNT attacks.

CONS:
- Unless you build a tunnel from a point on land to your underwater base, there's an obvious access issue and you'll need to invest heavily in potions of water breathing and depth strider.

If you choose an underwater base, build an access tunnel as well as some emergency underwater shelters in the area. Just one block of air can save your life if you run out of potion of water breathing or misjudge the distance.

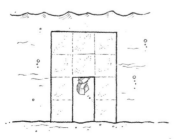

FIG. 15.
Emergency shelter providing air block refuge.

OUTER DEFENSES—DEFENDING YOUR TERRITORY

Regardless of design, your base must have tough outer defenses to keep unwelcome visitors from invading your space. We find the combination of a fire ditch or water moat, an outer perimeter wall and a range of base-wall defenses are enough to keep almost anything at bay.

FIRE DITCH

Netherrack just keeps burning once lit, so it's the perfect block to line the bottom of a fire ditch. The ditch should be at least three blocks wide to take care of any incoming hostile mobs.

FIG. 16.
Fire ditch. Sorry, hostile mobs.

MOAT DRAWBRIDGE

Use iron trapdoors to make a simple drawbridge over a two-block-wide water moat. It won't fool other players, who'll just raise the trapdoors to get across, but it'll be enough to dupe hostile mobs.

FIG. 17.i
This player wasn't born yesterday.

FIG. 17.ii
This creeper literally was.

PERIMETER WALL

Perimeter walls should have concealed or controlled points of entry—you don't want half the neighborhood barging into your territory. Multi-layered walls are best—add obsidian and water layers to help absorb explosions from creepers or TNT-wielding enemy players. Building a gravel or sand layer into the wall will annoy anyone trying to mine their way through. Obsidian floors will stop enemies digging a tunnel underneath your base to circumvent your walls.

Place a layer of lava in between two layers of stone wall. Anyone who tries to dig through is in for a lethal surprise.

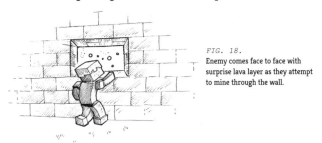

FIG. 18.
Enemy comes face to face with surprise lava layer as they attempt to mine through the wall.

A simple overhang will stop spiders from scaling your walls. Stop zombies and skeletons taking advantage of this feature to shelter from the sun by making the overhang out of glass blocks.

FIG. 19.
Glass overhang foils marauding arachnids as well as would-be shade bathers.

GOLEM DEFENDERS

Recruit some iron golems to help defend your perimeter walls. Remember to fence them in or attach them to a fence with a lead so they don't wander off. Their natural instinct is to destroy all hostile mobs on sight, except for the creeper, so they're very useful to have on your side. Just stack four solid blocks of iron in a T-shape, then put a pumpkin head on top to craft.

FIG. 20.
Alfred, the Survivors' resident iron golem.

Place snow golems in turrets protected by lava moats and position them along your perimeter wall so they can fire snowballs at approaching mobs. They'll be knocked backwards and distracted from pursuing you. Some mobs will even wander into the lava as they attempt to exact revenge on the snow golems.

FIG. 21.
Tina the snow golem, doing what she does best.

Just remember that snow golems won't last long in hot biomes like deserts and jungles, and will also perish if exposed to rain or other water sources. Adding a roof to each turret will help.

FINAL CHECKS
Don't forget to remove all trees and level all ground around your perimeter so you don't give mobs a leg-up over your wall.

FIG. 22.i
A well-tended perimeter.

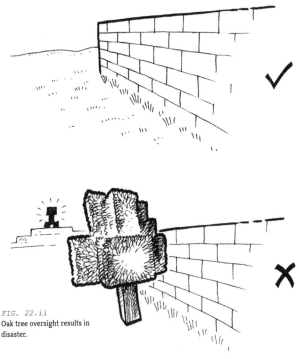

FIG. 22.ii
Oak tree oversight results in disaster.

BASE WALL DEFENSES

Walls should be manned and armed when possible. Watchtowers and walkways provide a platform for you and your allies to patrol as you scan the surrounding area for enemies. Build ammunition into your walls in the form of cannons or other projectile-launching devices so that you can fire on anything that gets too close.

Set up an alarm system using redstone, pressure plates and note blocks to warn you when monsters are approaching your door. This is a particularly handy way to ensure you're forewarned of the imminent arrival of near-silent mobs like creepers.

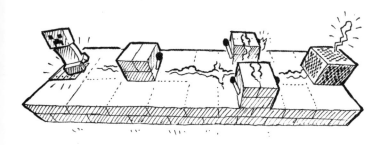

FIG. 23.
Alarm system being triggered by
unobservant creeper.

Spiders are the only hostile mob that can see you through glass, so build large windows to enable you to see what's happening outside.

Placing fences either side of your door allows you to shoot through the gap while preventing anything from getting through.

FIG. 24.
Sucks to be this spider right now.

AND FINALLY...

Carry out one final check to make sure there are no gaps in your base defenses. It can be easy to overlook vulnerabilities when you've been working on a design for a long time.

If you have the time and resources, build a decoy base nearby and hide your real base in a hill. This will keep any aspiring raiders occupied, at least for a while, allowing you to go about your business in peace.

Your actual base

Decoy base

FIG. 25.
Convincing decoy base setup.

THE ULTIMATE DEFENSE SYSTEM

Our ultimate defense system will protect your base and simultaneously demonstrate your cunning to would-be raiders. Use it as a starting point to develop your own system and intruders will seriously regret setting foot in your territory.

Piston chamber

Skeleton and spider chamber

Cobweb chamber

Lava pit

Zombie chamber

FIG. 26.
The ultimate defense system.

Soul sand and ice floor

Spider pit

Arrow run

Trapped chest End portal pit

Trapped chest lava pit

DEFENSIVE FEATURES

Let's look at the features of the system in more detail—you might want to copy our design or use it as inspiration to create your own. The single point of entry in your otherwise impenetrable outer walls will lead the raider into a small corridor, where they'll find what looks like a simple door and lever. Unfortunately for them it's not simple at all—unless they stand on the rear left block when pulling the lever, they won't be granted access to your base. Instead they'll drop down to a lower level where they'll be exposed to a series of painful and humiliating defensive features before being dispatched to a place from which they're unlikely to return.

COBWEB CHAMBER
A chamber full of cobwebs will reduce the raider's movement to almost nil, making progress to the exit frustratingly slow.

ZOMBIE CHAMBER
When trapped in a confined space with zombies, even the bravest raider will be shaken up.

FIG. 27.
Zombie chamber.

LAVA PIT
An agile raider may well be able to leap over this, but they'll land themselves in trouble if they fail.

26

PISTON CHAMBER
When triggered, the pressure plates in this chamber will activate strategically positioned sticky pistons that will pop up and block the raider's path. Another irritating setback.

SKELETON AND SPIDER CHAMBER
An episode inside this chamber, however brief, will leave your raider feeling rattled and vulnerable.

FIG. 28.
Skeleton and spider chamber.

SOUL SAND AND ICE FLOOR
Adding ice underneath soul sand dramatically increases the slowing effect—they're going to have a horribly slow time getting through this.

SPIDER PIT

Here, the raider has a choice: a run-in with a pit full of spiders, or another tediously slow struggle to push through the cobweb-strewn perimeter.

ARROW RUN

The raider will be able to dash through this chamber and make it to one of the doors at the other side if they're quick, but it'll cost them yet more precious health points as they'll be pelted with arrows as they go.

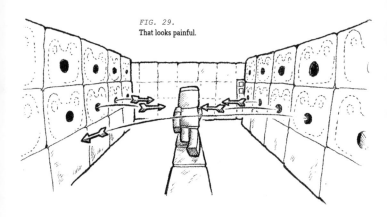

FIG. 29.
That looks painful.

By this point the cumulative effect of repeated attacks will have taken a considerable toll on the raider's nerves. And now for the best part...

TRAPPED CHEST LAVA PIT

When their greedy little eyes catch sight of this chest, the raider will believe they're on the verge of seizing your most valuable assets. But as soon as their thieving hands open the lid, the floor will disappear beneath their feet and they'll be deposited into a pit of lava.

TRAPPED CHEST END PORTAL PIT

The *pièce de résistance* of your defense system (assuming the raider didn't choose the trapped chest lava pit option) is another trapped chest which, when opened, will pull the floor out from under their feet and dispatch them directly through an End portal and into the End dimension. But not before they've fallen in excruciating slow motion through layer after layer of cobwebs, giving them plenty of time to contemplate the horror that awaits them on the other side.

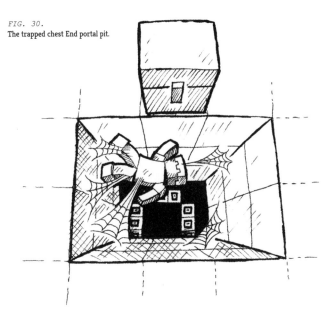

FIG. 30.
The trapped chest End portal pit.

You: 1
Raider: 0

BASE LAYOUT

So you've built a base, but it's not operational yet. Time to think about layout and contents. We'll let you in on the Survivors' open-plan base design—it's sure to inspire you.

ARSENAL PRODUCTION AND WORKSHOP

It's just common sense to group items together and store them logically, with armour in one chest, swords, bows and arrows in another, snowballs and eggs in another, etc.

Craft item frames and place them above each chest to indicate the contents. This makes it easy for you to collect what you need when you're short on time.

FIG. 31.
Clearly labeled item chests.

Set up a workshop area for crafting, smelting, forging and enchanting items as well as brewing potions. If you're part of a team you'll need several crafting tables, furnaces, anvils, enchantment tables (surrounded by bookshelves to allow access to higher-level enchantments), brewing stands and cauldrons.

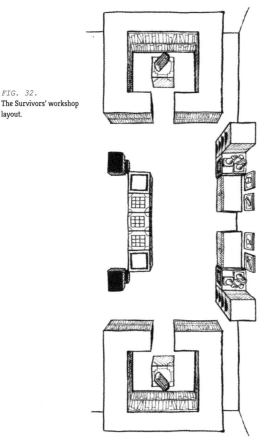

FIG. 32.
The Survivors' workshop layout.

BEACON BENEFITS

A beacon is the most expensive investment you're ever likely to make, but the benefits of having one in your base are enormous. The Survivors' beacon has saved our lives several times. When mounted on a pyramid it provides a powerful light source that can be seen from afar, as well as a range of beneficial status effects when you're in the vicinity.

As well as obsidian and glass you'll need a Nether star to craft a beacon, which means you'll have to take on the infamous wither boss. But we've seen that show before—see page 56 for our wither-defeating strategies.

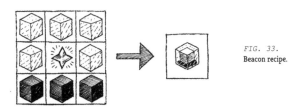

FIG. 33.
Beacon recipe.

There are four possible levels of pyramid—you'll either need 9, 34, 83 or 164 blocks. They can be built out of solid iron, gold, emerald or diamond blocks, or a combination of these, and must be positioned so that they have an unobstructed view of the sky. You'll also need to feed them an iron, gold or emerald ingot or a diamond. Yes, a diamond pyramid looks impressive, but its benefit is purely cosmetic and it doesn't provide any status effect advantages over a humble iron pyramid.

FIG. 34.
Level 1-4 pyramid structures.

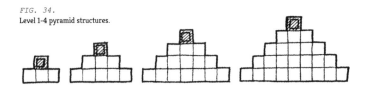

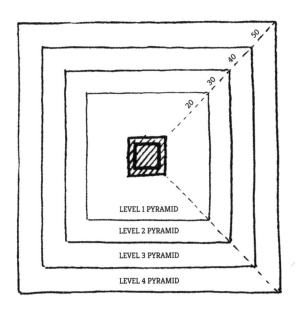

FIG. 35.
Diagram showing pyramid levels and
corresponding radius of status effects.

STATUS EFFECTS

A level 1 pyramid will provide status effects for a radius of 20 blocks.
Level 2 jumps to 30 blocks, level 3 is 40 and level 4 is 50. The beacon's
effects include speed (increases movement speed), haste (increases
mining speed), resistance (decreases incoming damage, level 2 pyramid
or higher), jump (increases jump height and distance, level 2 or higher),
strength (increases melee damage, level 3 or higher) and regeneration
(regenerates health, level 4 only). A level 4 pyramid allows you to select
two effects rather than one, and the effects will last longer as well as
being available over a greater distance.

RECOVERY ROOM

Build a recovery room in an easily accessible area of your base.

You'll need:

- A bed so you can sleep through the night. You won't be able to sleep if there are hostile mobs within ten blocks of your bed, so position it as far from your outer walls as possible.
- Plenty of food to restore your lost hunger points.
- A supply of golden apples.
- Buckets of milk to undo any negative status effects you may be suffering from.

We find music helps us relax—you might want to craft a jukebox so you have something to listen to as you recover.

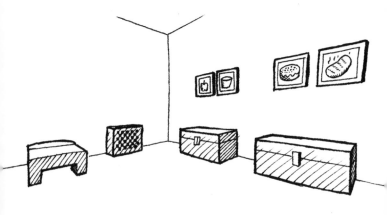

FIG. 36.
An exemplary recovery room,
guaranteed to make you feel better.

KITCHEN AND FARM

Some people get caught up in action and adventure and start to neglect their health. If you design your base to include a kitchen and farm area you'll be much more likely to have a supply of food at hand and look after yourself.

A crop farm should include wheat, carrots, potatoes, beetroot and sugar cane. This will give you everything you need to make baked goods, to craft hay bales to heal your horses and to attract and breed animals.

You'll also need a sustainable oak tree orchard to provide you with apples, whether you like them golden or otherwise.

Bone meal is a great fertilizer for most plants. Crafted from bones, it can be added to crops to speed up the growth process, so stock up on this to save time.

Next, you'll need to acquire some livestock for an animal farm. Track down at least two chickens, cows, pigs and sheep so that you have a supply of meat, eggs and milk. You'll also need horses for transport. Don't forget to breed them or you'll soon find your animal farm is empty.

Don't forget about complex baked goods like pumpkin pies and cake. These provide more food points than simple food items, and cake can be shared between several players at once.

FIG. 37.
Sweet treats.

IF YOUR WALLS ARE BREACHED

Even the most vigilant among us sometimes get raided by enemy players, and walls can be breached by hostile mobs, too. No matter how confident you are in your abilities, you should always prepare for the worst.

SECRET STORAGE ROOM

A secret storage room will reduce the chance of raiders clearing out your supplies or creepers blowing them up.

Single-block-wide doorways can be concealed by paintings—you'll need to place signs in the locations shown in fig. 38 to place the painting, and it may take a few tries to create one that's large enough.

FIG. 38.
Secret storage room under construction. Note the placement of signs.

You can also bury chests under your floors to make it even harder for raiders to loot your items.

If being raided is an unavoidable fact of life for you, create a secret, off-base store of materials. That way, if the worst happens and the raiders clean you out, at least you'll have some back-up materials to get you on your feet again.

FIG. 39.
Cutaway showing what looks like
a regular hill is actually packed
with supplies.

PANIC ROOMS

What do you do in truly critical situations when all that's left to do is panic? Fortunately there's a room for just such an occasion. Aptly named the Panic Room and installed under your base, it allows you to seal yourself off so intruders can't get at you without a great deal of time and effort.

They're an expensive investment—the walls, floor and ceiling should be crafted from obsidian to be blast-proof, and you'll need two more

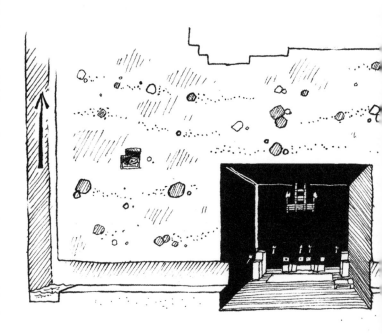

blocks of obsidian on hand to block the doorway from the inside and barricade yourself in.

Once built, fill your panic room with supplies—a light source, food, a bed, crafting materials and a crafting table.

You'll also need a cunning escape tunnel so you can resurface when the danger has passed. This could be a tunnel that takes you up to a hidden exit at ground level, a minecart system or a tunnel exit that's hidden behind a waterfall.

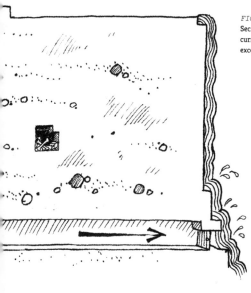

FIG. 40.
Secret blueprint of the Survivors' current panic room—yet to be used except in drills.

COMBAT
IN THE FIELD

VENIMUS
VIDIMUS
VICIMUS

WE CAME, WE SAW, WE CONQUERED

You may consider it a yawn-fest, but spending time getting the lay of the land allows you to identify potential areas for mining and development as well as any threats. Recon missions save lives, people.

GENERAL RECON MISSIONS

Spend some time finding and destroying or disabling monster spawners when setting up camp in a new area. Spawners are black, cage-like blocks that produce different mobs depending on their location—anything from zombies in dungeons and cave spiders in abandoned mineshafts to blazes in the Nether. Break the spawner with an iron pickaxe or, better, place torches next to and on top of it or cover it with lava. As an added bonus, you'll earn a nice chunk of experience for each spawner you destroy, and there's usually a chest full of loot nearby. If you choose to disable them with torches, hang around for a minute to be sure you did a thorough job and that it's definitely stopped spitting out mobs.

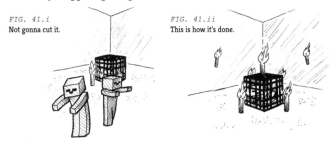

FIG. 41.i
Not gonna cut it.

FIG. 41.ii
This is how it's done.

It's also advisable to light up as much of the surrounding area as possible to reduce the number of monsters that spawn come nightfall.

Locate any terrain dangers such as ravines and natural lava pools, and mark them with torches or other recognizable blocks so you'll know when you're coming back to a potentially dangerous area.

If you discover an NPC village, don't be shy about using their resources–they'll be only too happy to help. Interact with villagers to see what they're willing to trade, help yourself to their crops and bookshelves and check out the contents of the blacksmith's chest. In return for taking all their supplies, you can help these simple folk fortify their village. It'll also reduce the chance of them being infected and turned into zombies, which will only add to your misfortunes. Build a wall around the village, light up any dark corners and, if they don't already have one, craft an iron golem to stand guard.

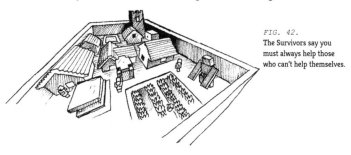

FIG. 42.
The Survivors say you must always help those who can't help themselves.

RAIDING ENEMY BASES
Raiding an enemy base for materials is both profitable and fun. If successful you'll replenish your own stores while simultaneously depleting your enemy's arsenal, and what could be more fun than that?

Your chances of success will be much greater if you do your recon first:

- Identify weaknesses in the base defenses that you could use as points of entry. Try tunneling underneath and breaking in through the floor.

- Take note of the equipment its occupants have–this will give you an idea of how much trouble you'll be in if you get into an altercation.

- Carry out the raid at night to reduce your chances of being spotted.

You'll need all your strength to defeat hostile mobs, but if you expect to stay one step ahead of them you'll need to use your brain, too. We've been studying the mobs since our Alpha days and have developed a threat-level grading system, from moderate to critical. Read on to discover our favorite tactics for taking them out.

ZOMBIES

Threat level:		MODERATE

HOME FRONT STRATEGIES
Build a ditch at least three blocks deep around your base. They'll fall right in and just aren't smart enough to get themselves out.

FIG. 43.
The ditch—simple yet effective.

Most people know you should use iron doors instead of wooden doors to prevent zombies breaking through, but as an added precaution we also like to place one block in front of the door, or raise the door a block above ground level. They can never figure it out and usually give up and wander away.

FIELD STRATEGIES

Position yourself on top of two dirt blocks and swing away—you'll be able to hit them but, much as they try, the zombies won't be able to reach you.

FIG. 44.
Player is tantalizingly close, yet just out of the zombies' reach.

Leave a small delay between hits. When zombies (or any other mobs) turn red it means they're already taking damage and are temporarily immune to further damage, so all you'll do is wear out your sword.

SKELETON

Threat level:		MODERATE

HOME FRONT STRATEGIES

As with zombies, your best bet is to dig a ditch around your base and wait for the brainless boneheads to fall in. When day comes, the sun will take care of the rest.

Fences will also stop skeletons crossing into your territory.

Make sure you place your doors from the outside, otherwise skeletons will be able to shoot through them.

Invest in a pack of wolves to chase skeletons away—you'll find them roaming around forest and taiga biomes and will need to tame them with bones to earn their loyalty.

FIG. 45.
Looks like spare ribs for dinner tonight.

FIELD STRATEGIES
Keep your ears open—you'll be able to hear skeletons approaching as they make a rattly sound when they move.

Use splash potion of health to harm them.

If you're in a cave during the day, lure the skeleton out into the sun.

SLIME

Threat level:		MODERATE

HOME FRONT STRATEGIES
Reduce the offending slime to tiny slimes, then give up and let them follow you around. They won't deal any damage at this size and can be fun to keep as pets.

FIG. 46.
Slime squad.

FIELD STRATEGIES
Position yourself between two blocks in a one-block-wide space. This leaves you free to attack the slime, but it won't be able to retaliate.

SILVERFISH

Threat level:		MODERATE

HOME FRONT STRATEGIES
When digging out an underground base, pay attention to the time it takes to mine each stone block. If it's taking longer than usual, it's a silverfish block and you'll need to stop immediately.

FIELD STRATEGIES
Silverfish drop nothing and aren't worth your time. The quickest way to get rid of them is to blow up the infested area with TNT, or barricade them into an enclosed area and pour lava on top of them.

FIG. 47.
Silverfish will imminently be engulfed in lava.

ENDERMITE

Threat level:		MODERATE

HOME FRONT STRATEGIES
Use soul sand around your perimeter—endermites will sink into it and suffocate.

FIG. 48.
Sorry, little guys.

FIELD STRATEGIES
Again, try blowing them all up with TNT. They don't drop anything useful and you really have better things to be doing.

GUARDIAN

Threat level:		MODERATE

HOME FRONT STRATEGIES
Unless you set up camp in the middle of an ocean monument, this isn't likely to be an issue.

FIELD STRATEGIES

Try hiding from guardians when they attack—they're not the brightest bulbs and will forget about you if you disappear from view.

FIG. 49.
Hide behind a pillar for long enough and a guardian will lose interest.

Their laser attack can penetrate armour to a certain extent, so invest in enchanted diamond armour before visiting an ocean monument.

CAVE SPIDER

Threat level:			MODERATE

HOME FRONT STRATEGIES

Avoid building your base underground, near an abandoned mineshaft, as this is where cave spiders spawn.

FIELD STRATEGIES

Your best bet is to go straight for the spawner and disable it. If that's not possible, stand on a two-block-high pillar and pour lava onto the offending arachnids.

FIG. 50.
Go caving, they said. It'll be fun, they said.

SPIDER

Threat level:		MODERATE

HOME FRONT STRATEGIES

Overhangs on your outer walls will stop spiders scuttling over the top.

Cacti walls are an excellent deterrent—place the cacti one block apart and spiders won't be able to get through. Instead they'll be forced to climb over, taking damage as they do.

FIG. 51.
Placement of cacti forces spiders over the top.

FIELD STRATEGIES

Try digging yourself a two-block-deep hole in the ground and hit the spider's underbelly as it stands above you.

SPIDER JOCKEY

Threat level:	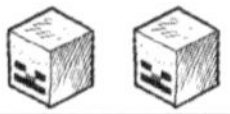	MODERATE

HOME FRONT STRATEGIES

Your wolves will help you deal with a spider jockey.

FIG. 52.
Wolves ganging up on a spider jockey.

FIELD STRATEGIES

Again, it's a good idea to take your wolves with you for backup. To be honest, it might also be a good idea to run away.

ENDERMAN

Threat level:		SUBSTANTIAL

HOME FRONT STRATEGIES

Create a minecart track around the perimeter of your base and set several carts going. If endermen approach, just nudge them towards the carts and they'll be scooped up and taken for a ride. They won't be able to teleport out of the cart once they're in it and then you can use them for archery practice.

FIG. 53.
Target acquired.

FIELD STRATEGIES

If possible, keep your eyes down. For some reason, wearing a pumpkin on your head allows you to look at them.

Build a dirt tower above your head so they can't hit you.

Build a two-block-high emergency enderman shelter. They won't be able to follow you inside, but you'll be able to hit them.

FIG. 54.
Emergency enderman shelter.

WITCH

Threat level:		SUBSTANTIAL

HOME FRONT STRATEGIES
If a witch approaches your base, position yourself on a high wall and shoot it with a bow and arrows.

Witches are pretty much immune to any kind of fire attack, so forget about using lava.

FIELD STRATEGIES

You need to move quickly and get the first hit in, then the witch will pause for a moment to heal itself. You'll know it's healing when it starts chugging potions. While this is going on it won't be able to attack you, so it's the perfect opportunity to get some more hits in.

FIG. 55.
Player hitting witch as it attempts to heal.

ELDER GUARDIAN

Threat level:					SEVERE

HOME FRONT STRATEGIES

Elder guardians will only be an issue on the home front if you have an underwater ocean base positioned near to a naturally occurring ocean monument. Avoid these areas and you should be fine.

FIELD STRATEGIES

Use pillars to shield yourself from their beam attack, and try to finish them off with an enchanted diamond sword. If you can, take a friend with you so one of you can sneak up behind the elder guardian while the other distracts it.

CREEPER

Threat level:		SEVERE

HOME FRONT STRATEGIES
Creepers are terrified of cats. Cats are extremely cute. Ergo, there's no reason not to invest in a whole bunch of cats. Get yourself over to your nearest jungle biome with some fish and tame as many ocelots as you can.

Set up a soul sand maze to slow creepers down.

FIG. 56.
Creeper being delayed by soul sand maze around base perimeter.

Build an obsidian pit to trap them.

A moat filled with water is another excellent creeper trap. The water will absorb the explosion if they detonate, potentially saving your base walls.

FIELD STRATEGIES
Try to block the explosion with your shield.

As with zombies, creepers' destructive plans can be thwarted if you stand on two dirt blocks and attack them from above. You can also try to suffocate them from this vantage point by dropping sand or gravel on their heads.

THE WITHER

Threat level:	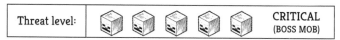	CRITICAL (BOSS MOB)

HOME FRONT STRATEGIES
Just don't spawn the wither anywhere near your base. Ever. Not even a little bit. Idea: try spawning one next to an enemy base then running away.

FIELD STRATEGIES
If you choose to spawn the wither out in the open, do it far away from all your valuables and ideally in an obsidian pit.

Start with ranged attacks with an enchanted bow (try power or punch enchantments), all the while downing potions of instant health and strength and eating golden apples. Once you've reduced the wither's health points, finish it off with an enchanted diamond sword. Smite and sharpness enchantments seem to produce the best results.

FIG. 57.
Keep your distance and use an enchanted bow
to reduce the wither's health before charging in
to finish it off with your sword.

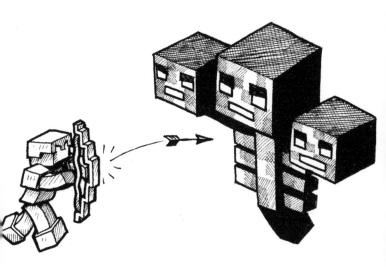

You could also try bringing along your wolves and snow and iron
golems, to act as distractions.

Enemy players are more unpredictable than hostile mobs, so you'll need to be particularly cunning to defeat them.

ONE-ON-ONE BATTLES

Tracking your enemy in the field requires stealth; you'll need to get as close as possible without them seeing you. Sneaking allows you to conceal your name so they won't spot you lurking behind blocks.

FIG. 58.
Sneak function being used to great effect.

Of course, our old friend the potion of invisibility will also ensure they don't see you coming.

This is where your recon pays off. If you know the land better than your opponent you'll be able to lead them into danger while keeping yourself safe.

Generally, it's best to go for the higher ground and rain critical hits on your opponent from above.

It's also possible to finish off an opponent by positioning yourself underneath them, however. Try hiding in a hole in the ground and hitting their legs from below.

Remember to eat, but don't waste your food—wait until you've lost at least eight food points before breaking out the pork chops. Nobody likes a greedy guts.

SMALL GROUPS
Working as part of a small group of three or four people gives you the perfect opportunity to test out the art of misdirection.

Split your group into two. The first group should position themselves in caves overlooking a ravine. The second group heads out to take on an enemy group. Mid-battle, the second group should retreat into the ravine, bringing the enemy group in range of the hidden group. Back them into a corner and finish them off with the help of your allies.

FIG. 59.
Nowhere to hide.

LARGE GROUPS

Tackling enemy players as a larger team will maximize your chances of success as you'll be able to perform more complex maneuvers for devastating effect.

Within your team you should have a variety of functions: archers, potion-lobbers and a small number of what we call juggernauts (heavily enchanted players who can deal incredible damage) as well as regular armed players. Regardless of the maneuver you use, having all these elements within your ranks will really help you gain the upper hand.

THE PINCER

Attack the opposing team from two sides so that they're surrounded and forced into a small, enclosed space.

Enemy group surrounded and
being forced into small space.

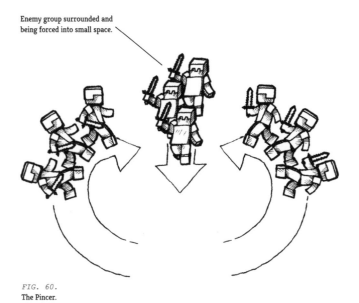

FIG. 60.
The Pincer.

THE AMBUSH

Take half your group out into the field to take on an enemy group, and instruct the other half to hide nearby. When the opposing team thinks they're winning, it's time for the hidden group to emerge and attack from the side. They'll never see it coming, and everybody knows you can't win a war on two fronts.

FIG. 61.
The Ambush.

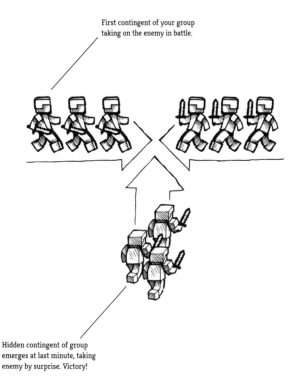

First contingent of your group taking on the enemy in battle.

Hidden contingent of group emerges at last minute, taking enemy by surprise. Victory!

And now for a few tips on the art of winning combos.

A combo is achieved when you score a succession of hits against an opponent, without the opponent having the opportunity to retaliate or hit you back.

The following combos are guaranteed to get results and ensure your enemies know not to mess with you again.

THE TRIPLE THREAT

STEP 1
Throw a fire charge at the block under your opponent's feet to get them all hot and bothered, then swing at them with your fire aspect sword.

FIG. 62.i
Opponent finds feet are suddenly on fire while simultaneously receiving fire aspect sword in face.

STEP 2

Throw a splash potion of harming at your opponent's face to further exacerbate the situation for them while protecting yourself with your shield.

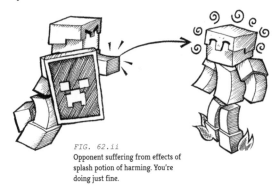

FIG. 62.ii
Opponent suffering from effects of splash potion of harming. You're doing just fine.

STEP 3

Step back to avoid singeing yourself, then pelt your opponent with arrows from your trusty bow to finish the job.

FIG. 62.iii
Arrow piercing armour and reducing opponent's health points to nil.

THE STAB IN THE BACK

STEP 1
Once you're sure they intend to fight you, teleport behind your opponent using an ender pearl.

FIG. 63.i
Arrival at prime vantage point behind
bewildered opponent.

STEP 2
Apply lava to opponent using a lava bucket.

FIG. 63.ii
Opponent is clearly overwhelmed
by lava.

STEP 3
Teleport behind opponent once more, and finish off with fire aspect and
knockback sword just as opponent turns around again.

FIG. 63.iii
Sword makes contact with
infuriated opponent, reducing
their health points to nil.

THE FAKE-OUT

STEP 1
Hide your enchanted diamond equipment. Instead, strike out at your opponent with an iron sword, then turn and run as if you have no actual idea what you're doing.

FIG. 64.i
Runner flailing around, creating a convincing air of panic.

STEP 2
Make for a deadly ravine nearby that only you know about. Try to jump about a bit to keep their attention on you and not on where they're going.

FIG. 64.ii
Clear path being made towards
treacherous cliff. Opponent is oblivious.

STEP 3
Use an ender pearl to teleport behind your opponent, switch to knockback diamond sword and hit your opponent, pushing them over the ledge and into the ravine.

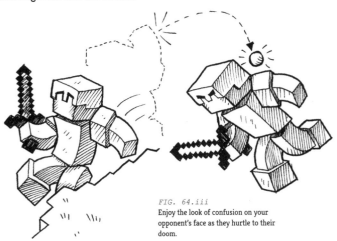

FIG. 64.iii
Enjoy the look of confusion on your opponent's face as they hurtle to their doom.

67

When things aren't going your way, there's no shame in a tactical retreat.

ONE-ON-ONE BATTLES

Use third-person view to see over obstacles you're hiding behind—this way you can take a look around without moving and revealing yourself.

FIG. 65.
Player wisely using third-person view to scope out area ahead.

In critical situations, dig three blocks into the ground, jump in, then place a glass block above your head. You'll be safe for a little while.

If you get pushed off a cliff during a fight, use ender pearls to teleport or a water bucket to break your fall.

If you're trapped in a small space and there's a stream of water or lava coming right at you, place a ladder or sign on the side of the block in front of you to stop the flow. This buys you time to devise a cunning exit strategy.

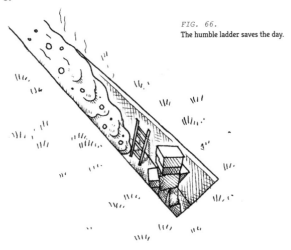

FIG. 66.
The humble ladder saves the day.

Riding a horse allows you to cover ground much more quickly and jump low obstacles such as fences.

Ender pearls can be used to teleport away from an onslaught. Potion of swiftness will also allow you to make a speedy departure.

The Nether dimension is a horrifying place, filled with lava and highly dangerous hostile mobs. Unfortunately, you can't avoid it—it's home to many valuable items that can't be found in the Overworld. Use our strategies to stay safe down under and defeat these hellish creatures.

FIRST THINGS FIRST

Build a glass enclosure around your Nether portal as soon as you arrive. This allows you to look around for hostile mobs, but also keeps your portal safe from ghast fireballs since they won't be able to see you.

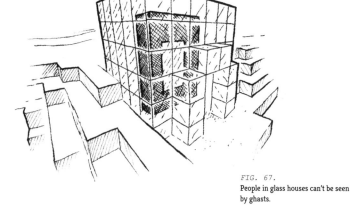

FIG. 67.
People in glass houses can't be seen by ghasts.

If you're planning to spend a significant amount of time in the Nether, build a small shelter so you have somewhere to retreat. Also consider repurposing a Nether fortress for your own needs. Simply block off the blaze spawners, repair the outer walls and bridges and fill it with supplies, and it'll be positively homely.

Nether fortresses are vast, and the long, barren corridors all look the same in the gloomy light. When exploring Nether fortresses, place torches on the left walls as you go, so you can turn around and follow them back out again. Be extra cautious when turning corners as you're likely to come face-to-face with a hostile mob.

ZOMBIE PIGMAN

Threat level:			MODERATE

STRATEGIES FOR DEFEAT:

Push them off one of the Nether's many cliffs.

Suffocate them with sand or gravel.

Blow them up with TNT. This can work particularly well with a group.

FIG. 68.
Well, that was rash.

71

Don't bother with lava—zombie pigmen are immune to fire-based attacks.

Stand on a three-block-high pillar and hit them from above.

BLAZE

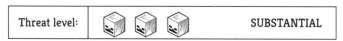

Threat level:		SUBSTANTIAL

STRATEGIES FOR DEFEAT:

Use the location of the spawner—at the top of a staircase—to your advantage. Block off the staircase, leaving a half-block gap for you to hit through, then wait for the blazes to come at you.

FIG. 69.
Clever use of space to defeat blazes.

Drink a potion of fire resistance.

Pelt them with snowballs.

Alternatively, cast a fishing rod in their direction and reel them towards you, then finish them off with an enchanted diamond sword.

GHAST

Threat level:		SUBSTANTIAL

STRATEGIES FOR DEFEAT:

If possible, use its size against it and trap it in an enclosed space or corner inside a Nether fortress, then finish it off with an enchanted diamond sword.

Reel it in on a fishing rod, then finish it off with your sword.

Hide behind a wall of blocks and shoot at the ghast around the sides with a bow and arrows. Ghasts only shoot fireballs at you if they can see you.

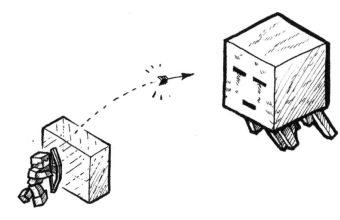

FIG. 70.
Wall being used as a shield during
ghast fight.

73

WITHER SKELETON

| Threat level: | | SUBSTANTIAL |

STRATEGIES FOR DEFEAT:

Cram yourself into a two-block-high space and swing at their legs and body. They won't be able to follow you inside.

Stand on a three-block-high pillar and hit them with an enchanted sword.

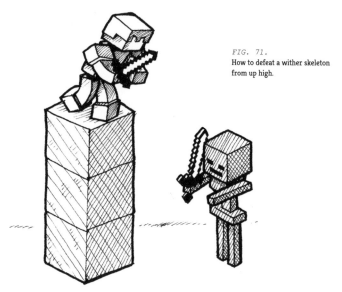

FIG. 71.
How to defeat a wither skeleton from up high.

Blow them up with TNT.

MAGMA CUBE

Threat level:		SUBSTANTIAL

STRATEGIES FOR DEFEAT:

Get to higher ground and shoot them with a bow and arrows.

FIG. 72.
Player wisely shooting a magma cube from higher ground.

Push them over a cliff by hitting them with a knockback sword.

THE END GAME

So you thought the Nether was bad? The End dimension is the most dangerous place you'll ever visit, but, if you can defeat the ender dragon, it's also the most rewarding. The dragon is the ultimate hostile mob—many have tried to defeat it and many have failed. We're among the few who have succeeded, so pay very close attention to the next few pages if you intend to try it yourself.

FIRST THINGS FIRST

The End is also inhabited by endermen. You'll either need to wear a pumpkin head or muster all your self-control and keep your eyes on the ground.

Consider building an underground bunker complete with crafting table, furnace and chest so you can craft more weapons.

Take an emergency stack of obsidian so you can build a panic shelter if the fight isn't going your way.

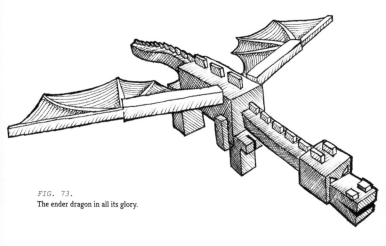

FIG. 73.
The ender dragon in all its glory.

THE ENDER DRAGON

Threat level:	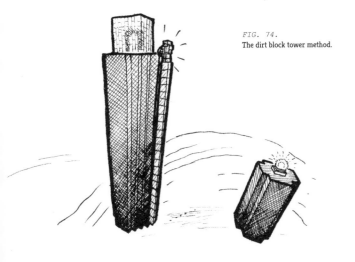	CRITICAL (BOSS MOB)

The ender dragon shoots dragon's breath at its targets—a putrid, acidic substance that deals damage to anything unfortunate enough to be on the receiving end—as well as exploding fireballs.

STRATEGIES FOR DEFEAT:

Destroy the crystals first. The crystals on the tallest pillars are surrounded by cages. These cages can't be destroyed by arrows, so you'll be forced to climb up the pillars. Try using ladders or tower your way up using dirt blocks—using an easily mineable block like dirt ensures you can mine your way back down again quickly.

FIG. 74.
The dirt block tower method.

The dragon will instinctively protect the pillars, swooping to attack once you begin to climb. If you make it to the top of the pillars, don't hang about once you've destroyed the crystals. Although you may think the higher vantage point will give you an edge, you'll lose a dangerous number of health points if the dragon knocks you off. Which it will.

You'll know you're making progress when the dragon comes down to the podium in the center of the pillars—when this happens, it's time to get out your enchanted bow and arrows. If you can, aim at its head rather than its body as it takes more damage there.

Now, what I'm about to divulge might surprise you: our go-to weapon of choice to finish off the dragon is the humble bed. Beds have been designed to explode if you try to sleep in them in the Nether or End dimensions, so place one on the ground at a strategic moment, try to sleep in it and it will detonate right in the dragon's face. This will deal more damage than a TNT explosion, so ensure you don't blow yourself up in the process by placing an obsidian block between yourself and the bed to absorb some of the blast. It'll take several beds to finish the dragon off so make sure you have a good supply—ten is advisable.

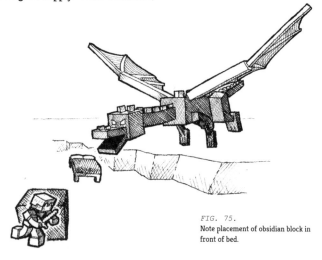

FIG. 75.
Note placement of obsidian block in front of bed.

Once the dragon has been defeated you'll be rewarded with an enormous amount of experience points, plus the coveted dragon egg trophy. Do not mine it. Use pistons to push the egg off its plinth, but cover the End portal first so it doesn't drop through.

We recently learned that you can respawn the dragon once you've defeated it. Craft four ender crystals, then place one on each side of the End exit portal and the dragon will poof back into your life.

FIG. 76.
How to summon the ender dragon
for round two.

END EXPLORATION

The End dimension is vast and there are many other islands to explore—your victorious defeat of the dragon is just the beginning of your End adventure.

It won't escape your attention that the End gateway (the gateway that appears when you defeat the dragon) is only one block high and wide, and not big enough for a person to travel through. Throw an ender pearl through it, though, and you'll be transported to the outer islands.

As you set out to explore the outer islands, leave a trail of markers (e.g. torches or cobblestone blocks) from your portal location—everything looks the same on these islands and it's easy to get lost.

End cities, found on the outer islands, are home to a number of valuable materials, including elytra—wings that allow you to glide through the air—and End rods—decorative, light-emitting items. Explore all the towers you come across to locate the loot.

Be careful as you explore—End cities are crawling with hostile shulkers.

SHULKER

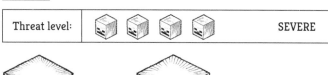

Threat level:		SEVERE

FIG. 77.i
The shulker with shell closed.

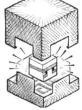

FIG. 77.ii
The shulker with shell open.

Shulkers (or shell-lurkers) are small, pesky creatures that blend in with their surroundings, making it easy for them to take you by surprise. The hard, outer shell protects the creature inside and they have the ability to teleport.

They shoot target-seeking projectiles that inflict two hearts of damage and a levitation effect. It might not sound like the most dangerous effect, but you're likely to be several blocks high when it wears off and the fall can kill you.

If you're careful, the levitation effect can be used to your advantage— you'll be able to traverse the voids between islands to get to a new location quickly and easily.

STRATEGIES FOR DEFEAT:

Knock the shulker projectiles off course with a sword.

Shulkers take more damage when their shell is open, so get some critical hits in when the fleshy, white creature peeps out of the shell.

FIG. 78.
Player skilfully knocking shulker projectile off course with diamond sword.

PRO CHALLENGE
SPEED RUN TO THE END

So you've learned plenty of valuable secrets—now it's time to challenge yourself with a speed run to the End. As our final gift to you we'll share our tactics for completing the ultimate mission in the shortest possible time.

If you're attempting this as a team, divide the tasks listed in the following pages between you, but make sure everyone has a supply of weapons and beds.

EQUIPMENT

Iron shovel	Shears
Iron pickaxe	Bow and arrows
Iron axe	Golden apples
Flint and steel	At least 4 beds
Boat	Emeralds
Diamond sword	Eyes of ender
Diamond pickaxe	Obsidian

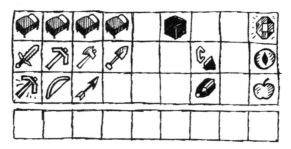

FIG. 79.
Speed-run-ready inventory.

STRATEGY

Ideally, you need to start in a village near to an open cave system and a stronghold. This puts you in the vicinity of several necessary materials, including flint (as pathways are often made from gravel), tools and weapons, armour, apples, various ores and obsidian (found in village chests).

You need to move quickly. Jumping as you run around will increase your speed, and you can gather food as you go—use a flint and steel to kill animals and they'll drop cooked meat, ready to be eaten.

Remember to use a boat if you need to travel across any large bodies of water as it'll get you there much more quickly.

Time to make friends with the local villagers:

Brown-robed fletchers trade bows and arrows. Not all brown-robed villagers are fletchers, so you may need to try a few before you find the right one.

Purple-robed clerks trade eyes of ender for emeralds in the third tier of trading. To unlock this tier you'll need to trade with them twice.

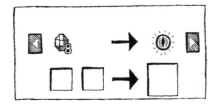

FIG. 80.
A clerk's third-tier trading screen.

Track down some sheep—they can often be found roaming around village perimeters. You'll need two iron ingots to craft shears, which will allow you to collect wool from the sheep and use it to craft beds.

You'll need to make a quick visit to the Nether. You're unlikely to have enough obsidian for a portal at this stage, but you can make obsidian by flowing water into a lava source block. Try using the lava outside the village blacksmith, or find a surface lava pool and create a waterfall next to it. Remember, you'll need a diamond pickaxe to mine the obsidian you create.

FIG. 81.
How to make obsidian, no caving required.

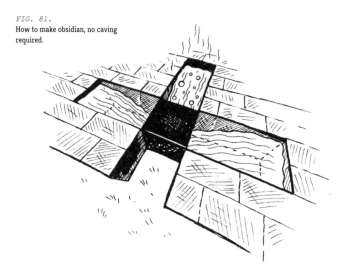

Once in the Nether, use cobblestone to make stepping stones across any soul sand beaches—as you know, walking on soul sand will really slow you down.

Find the Nether fortress and head for the blaze spawner. Collect blaze rods by blocking off the staircase and hitting the blazes through a half-block gap—see page 72 for a reminder.

You can use the Nether to shortcut your way to the stronghold in the Overworld if it's far away from your village, since one block in the Nether equals eight blocks in the Overworld.

Make your way to the stronghold. Check all chests you come across as you search for the End portal room. If you're lucky you may find eyes of ender in one of the stronghold chests—you'll need these to activate the portal.

If you pass a stronghold library, destroy the cobwebs to stock up on string so you can craft spare bows.

You'll need to defeat some endermen to collect the rest of the twelve eyes needed to activate the portal.

Once in the portal room, fill the empty portal slots with eyes of ender (several will already be filled).

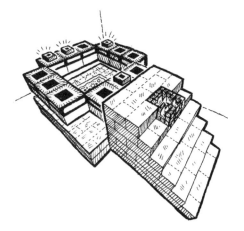

FIG. 82.
An incomplete End portal.

Once you reach the End, follow our previous instructions to defeat the dragon. I don't mean to brag, but we've finished it off using just four beds. That's what we call the Survivors' Special.

DEBRIEFING

VERBA
VOLANT
SCRIPTA
MANENT

SPOKEN WORDS FLY AWAY, WRITTEN WORDS REMAIN

FINAL NOTES

I trust you found our Book of Secrets valuable and have learned plenty of new survival strategies. To ensure our knowledge is passed on to other worthy recipients, you'll need to hide the book somewhere new, for another deserving survivor to find.

We've left the next few pages blank for you to add your own notes—hopefully you can teach the next reader some tricks of your own.

All that's left for us to do is to wish you luck on your adventures—but with secrets like these up your sleeve, you probably don't need it.

Hit upon creative new ways to kill hostile mobs? Note them down here.

_____

_____

_____

_____

_____

_____

_____

_____

Note down your ingenious inventions here.

_____

_____

_____

_____

_____

_____

_____

_____

_____

_____

_____

_____

_____

_____

_____

FINAL NOTES

Make a record of your best PVP moves.

_____

_____

_____

_____

_____

_____

_____

_____

_____

_____

_____

_____

_____

_____

_____

_____

_____

_____

Devised a brilliant defense system for your base? Explain the features and sketch it out here.

_____

_____

_____

_____

_____

_____

_____

_____

_____

_____

_____

_____

_____

_____

_____

FINAL NOTES

Record your best Nether and End dimension strategies here.

FINAL NOTES

What are your sneakiest raid tactics?

_____

_____

_____

_____

_____

_____

_____

_____

_____

_____

_____

_____

_____

_____

_____

FINAL NOTES

Explain and sketch your most successful traps here.

_____

_____

_____

_____

_____

_____

_____

_____

_____

_____

_____

_____

_____

_____

FINAL NOTES

Detail your most notable team victories.

_____

_____

_____

_____

_____

_____

_____

_____

_____

_____

_____

_____

_____

_____

_____

_____

_____

FINAL NOTES

What were your best solo victories?